#*GRAD*

A Grad School Survival Guide

BOSS

2nd Edition

DR. TOYIN ALLI

Published byThe Academic Society LLC

www.theacademicsociety.com

ISBN: 979-8-9931928-2-6

Second Edition

Printed in the United States of America

Book layout prepared for print via Amazon Kindle Direct Publishing (KDP)

First printing: July 2019

For permissions, speaking inquiries, or bulk order information, contact: support@theacad emicsociety.com

Praise for #GRADBOSS: A Grad School Survival Guide & The Academic Society

Great quick read for grad students

"This is a great, quick read for incoming and current grad students who are struggling to keep it all together. Toyin has been there, so she gets it. Would highly recommend to all incoming grad students."

Alice, PhD Student

Supporting a new era of graduate students and academics!

"This is a practical guide that helps break things down into actionable steps. It is especially helpful for students who haven't always had guidance or support in pursuing academic degrees. Alternatively, if you have received good academic support, it will help guide you through the changes of our generation. This guide is digestible, easy to follow, and provides great advice!"

Mary, Master's Student

The support I so badly needed

"I now feel empowered to make decisions about my life and grad school that are right for me; I have more clarity about how I want to spend my time and the kind of professional I'm growing to be; and I've been able to extend the support that I so badly needed to others and actually make an impact on their journey. My advisor told me yesterday that my collaborator RAVED about my new project at the student evaluation meetings, and I couldn't imagine getting to this point where I'm excited about my future, so supported and encouraged to reach my goals, and constantly learning so much - without this group and all the energy, time, effor, enthusiasm, and kindness you put into it. Thank you!"

Katherine, PhD Student

A Letter to the Reader

Dear Grad Student,

First of all, take a breath.

If no one has told you yet—*you're doing amazing*. Simply by being here, reading this book, and choosing to invest in your grad school experience, you're showing up for yourself in a big way. That matters. And I'm so glad you're here.

Grad school can be a beautiful, life-changing chapter. But it can also be disorienting, isolating, and exhausting. There are deadlines, expectations, unspoken rules, and a constant feeling that you should be doing more, even when you're already doing *everything*.

When I was a grad student, I got an incomplete in a class my very first semester. It was humbling, confusing, and honestly, a little embarrassing. But it also became a turning point. I created structure. I built systems. I asked for help. And slowly, I started to thrive... not just survive. That experience helped me graduate with my PhD in five years, land my dream teaching job, and eventually create The Academic Society: a cozy corner of the internet where grad students could find clarity, community, and calm.

This book, *the second edition of #GRADBOSS*, was created with that same intention.

It's not about being perfect. It's about learning how to trust yourself, manage your time without guilt, build a life outside of your program, and find joy *while* getting your degree. Inside, you'll find stories from real students, simple strategies you can implement today, and reflection prompts to help you stay grounded and intentional throughout your journey.

Whether you're a first-year master's student just finding your footing or a doctoral candidate trying to make it to the finish line—I wrote this for you.

I want you to finish this book feeling seen, supported, and empowered to define success on your own terms. Because being a #GRADBOSS isn't about doing it all. It's about doing what matters, with confidence and care.

You've got this. And I've got you.

With so much encouragement,

Dr. Toyin Alli

Founder of The Academic Society

How to Use This Book

This isn't a book you have to read cover to cover in one sitting (though you totally can). Think of it as a *survival guide meets journal meets pep talk*. It's here for you in every season of grad school—whether you're just starting out, hitting a mid-semester slump, or trying to get unstuck in your writing.

Here's how to make the most of it:

Read it like a conversation.

This isn't a textbook. You'll find stories, strategies, and reminders that you're not alone. My tone is casual and supportive on purpose—because grad school doesn't need to feel more formal than it already is.

Use the prompts.

Throughout the book, you'll find guided reflection prompts, planning pages, and self-assessments. These are here to help you think, process, and personalize your strategy. Grab a notebook, open your favorite notes app, or use the downloadable planner linked in the Resources section.

Skip around as needed.

Each chapter stands on its own. Need help managing unstructured time? Flip to Chapter 8. Feeling isolated? Try Chapter 12. Having advisor stress? Head to Chapter 13. Let this guide meet you where you are.

Revisit it regularly.

You'll grow in ways you can't even imagine. Come back to this book each semester, each transition, or each time you hit a wall. New lessons will land differently as you evolve.

Pair it with the podcast.

I've included QR codes in the Resources section linking to the *Grad School Stories* private podcast—a companion series of real student voices sharing what it's *really* like to be in grad school right now.

Use what serves you. Leave the rest. Adapt it to your life and learning style. That's what a #GRADBOSS does.

A Note for Educators & Mentors

If you're reading this as a professor, program director, McNair mentor, or advisor—thank you. Your presence here says a lot about your commitment to supporting graduate students beyond the syllabus or lab.

This book is designed not just for students, but for the learning environments around them. We know that success in graduate school isn't just about coursework or research. It's about mindset, structure, support, and wellbeing. That's what *#GRADBOSS* addresses head-on.

Suggested Uses in Academic Programming:

- As a *summer prep read* for incoming grad cohorts or McNair Scholars

- As part of *first-year experience courses* or orientation workshops

- As a *reflection tool* during advising meetings or writing retreats

- As a *framework* for time management seminars or support groups

- As a *community builder* for peer mentoring or cohort development

Each chapter includes real stories, actionable strategies, and discussion-ready prompts that can be used in small group settings or individual reflection. There's also a "How to Use This Book With a Grad Cohort" guide in the back for easy implementation.

If you're using this book with a group of students, feel free to reach out at support@theacademicsociety.com for bonus materials or bulk pricing.

You're not just guiding students through a program, *you're shaping who they become*. And we're honored to support that work.

What It Means to Be a #GRADBOSS

The term *#GRADBOSS* was born out of a simple idea: what if grad school didn't have to feel like survival mode?

In the online business world, people use the word "boss" to describe someone who's in control of their life and work—someone who sets boundaries, owns their time, and leads with confidence. I wanted that energy for grad students. And that's how the #GRADBOSS identity came to life.

A #GRADBOSS is:

- A student who takes ownership of their experience

- Someone who's productive *and* prioritizes rest

- A person who sets goals *and* makes space for joy

- A builder of community... even when things feel isolating

- A leader who lifts others up and sets a new standard for balance

Being a #GRADBOSS doesn't mean you never feel overwhelmed. It means you have tools to *come back to yourself* when you do. It means you create systems that support your success, without losing who you are in the process.

It's not about being the best. It's about being the most *you*. Let that be your compass.

Meet the
#GRADBOSSes

G rad school can feel like uncharted territory. But here's a message for you. You're not alone, and you don't have to figure it all out by yourself.

When I began writing this second edition of *#GRADBOSS: A Grad School Survival Guide*, I knew I didn't want it to be just my story. I wanted this book to reflect the diversity of experiences, identities, and voices that make up today's graduate student community. So, I invited six incredible students (members of my *#GRADBOSS Learning Community*) to share their journeys with you.

Each of these students brings something unique to the table. Different fields, different paths, different strengths. But all of them have embraced the mindset of a #GRADBOSS: someone who takes ownership of their experience, prioritizes their well-being, and builds a life beyond just the degree.

You'll see their stories throughout the book, quoted and referenced in the chapters ahead. But you can also hear directly from them on the Grad School Stories private podcast—a companion to this book where I share even more interviews, behind-the-scenes reflections, and practical encouragement. You'll find access instructions in the Resources

section at the back of the book and theacademicsociety.com/gradbo
ss-book-gifts.

For now, meet the grad students who helped shape this edition.
You'll see pieces of yourself in their stories, and new possibilities, too.

Student Spotlight: Lynn

Field: Clinical Mental Health Counseling, **School:** Lindsay Wilson University

"A #GRADBOSS is someone who balances their grad life and real life—and still makes it happen without losing their peace."

Lynn's grad school journey didn't follow a straight line. After swearing off school following a tough undergraduate experience, he returned years later as a fully self-motivated adult learner—armed with life experience, certifications, and a commitment to do things differently.

Now a full-time adviser working with foster youth by day and a graduate student by night, Lynn thrives by using systems: chunking assignments, working smarter (not harder), and keeping his community close through Facebook and Discord. His story is a powerful reminder that the "nontraditional" path often leads to the most profound success.

Student Spotlight: Addie

Field: Psychology, **School:** Rutgers University

"You were admitted into the program. You're not supposed to be a professional or expert—you fully belong here."

Addie entered grad school with a strong academic foundation and an early awareness of imposter syndrome—but she didn't let that stop her. From day one, she intentionally sought out support, tuning into The Academic Society's YouTube channel and joining the #GRADBOSS community before her program even began.

Her quiet confidence and emotional insight shine through as she shares how redefining success helped her let go of perfectionism and focus on purpose. Addie's story encourages new students to trust their preparation, seek out aligned mentorship, and embrace the learning curve with grace.

Student Spotlight: Asha

Field: Liturgical and Sacramental Theology, **School:** Catholic University of America

"Taking a break isn't counterproductive—it's how I get my best ideas."

Asha's path to grad school was unconventional. After a successful career in IT, she transitioned to theological study and discovered her passion for bridging historical knowledge with lived faith. As a mother, student, and scholar, Asha models how intentional rest, reflection, and self-awareness sustain long-term growth.

From studying four languages to moving across states with her family, her story reveals what it means to lead with both purpose and flexibility. For Asha, being a #GRADBOSS is about agency—the freedom to work hard *and* rest well.

Student Spotlight: Briana

Field: Disease Ecology, **School:** University of Texas at Austin

"You may do things you never realized you're capable of doing. Make space for that."

Briana's story is one of resilience, adaptability, and quiet power. When her research path shifted—first due to advisor changes, then due to the pandemic—she embraced the unknown and discovered new areas of strength. Over time, she grew into her role as a subject matter expert, learning to trust herself even when the path looked unfamiliar.

Now a postdoc and mentor in the #GRADBOSS community, Briana encourages students to explore the parts of grad school that surprise them and to find joy in the process—even when it's imperfect.

Student Spotlight: Asya

F **ield:** Policy Analysis, **School:** Pardee RAND Graduate School
"I deserve to be here. I choose to be here. And I will always make decisions that are in my best interest."

Asya's journey includes two graduate degrees, moments of doubt, and incredible growth. After leaving one PhD program with a master's, she redefined her version of success, found healing through therapy, and stepped into a new identity as a data professional and teacher.

She reminds us that rest, clarity, and self-trust are vital. Her advice to other students? Be bold about your needs. Normalize support. And never let anyone else define your success for you.

Student Spotlight: Cristina

Field: Health Promotion & Behavioral Science, **School:** San Diego State University

"Being a #GRADBOSS means being open to mistakes, staying resilient, and lifting others up as you grow."

Cristina's story is one of grace, growth, and grounded community. After five years away from school, she returned to grad school with a renewed sense of purpose—and graduated with all A's. But it wasn't just the grades that mattered. It was how she redefined success, learned to manage perfectionism, and discovered how deeply community-centered her path really was.

As a research coordinator working in public health, Cristina already had experience leading projects, mentoring undergrads, and managing teams. Her grad program supported that growth, but it also challenged her to let go of rigid expectations, trust her process, and be kind to herself through moments of self-doubt. Impostor syndrome didn't disappear, but she learned to recognize it, work through it, and recover with grace.

Cristina reminds us that taking time off before grad school isn't a setback—it's often the very thing that makes us more ready. She entered her program with a clear "why," and it became her anchor through every challenge. Her advice? Don't be afraid to build community outside your cohort, share what you're learning, and trust that mistakes are part of rising to a new level.

Contents

Part I: Own Your Experience

Build confidence, clarity, and an identity you won't lose in the process.

Chapter One

Welcome to Grad School, Welcome to You

*T**he truth about what grad school is really like and how to reclaim your power from the very beginning.*

A Gentle Truth

When I started grad school, I thought I was ready.

I had the GPA. I had the ambition. I had been accepted into a PhD program in mathematics, which felt like an enormous achievement as a Black woman from Mississippi. But within the first semester, that confidence started to crack.

I remember orientation week. Some students were encouraged to take a couple of undergraduate-level courses to build a stronger foundation before diving into grad-level math. And a lot of us were... *offended*.

Take undergrad classes? **Do you not think I'm smart enough for graduate coursework?** I'll prove you wrong.

But instead of pushing back, I listened and I'm so glad I did.

I took two split-level undergraduate classes that first semester, and I thrived. I was the star student. I made A's on everything. And being a first year graduate student struggling with imposter syndrome, it was exactly what I needed to rebuild my confidence. Honestly?

I don't know if I would've felt like I belonged in grad school without those classes.

But the real turning point came in the other two courses I took that semester: abstract algebra and topology. I got a B in algebra. And in topology? *I got an incomplete.*

The Incomplete That Taught Me Everything

Topology is one of the hardest math subjects out there. It's a notoriously abstract area of mathematics, and one that wasn't even offered at my undergraduate institution. I walked into that classroom already behind. I had no prior exposure to the concepts, no intuitive understanding of the content, and no roadmap for how to study at that level.

And I wasn't alone in struggling. I'll never forget one day after a test when our professor wrote all of the exam scores on the board, not with names, but just as numbers. He split them into two columns: passing and non-passing.

My score was at the top of the non-passing column.

That moment stung. It was humbling and deeply uncomfortable. I kept showing up, kept trying, but I knew I wasn't grasping the material. I probably would have ended the course with a C—a grade that, in grad school, feels a lot like failure.

But instead of giving me that C, my professor gave me something else: **mercy**. He gave me an incomplete.

Now, that might sound like a lifeline but make no mistake: an incomplete is work. I had to spend the entire next semester meeting with him weekly, proving every theorem we had covered in class. On the board. One by one.

It was horrible. I cried more than once. It felt like academic bootcamp.

But by the end, I wasn't just proving theorems. I was learning how to learn at the graduate level. I stopped just "doing the problems." I started studying the ideas behind them. I learned how to think like a mathematician, not just a student.

That incomplete was my breaking point and my breakthrough. After that semester, I never earned below a B in grad school again. Not because I got smarter. But because I knew what it actually took to succeed.

Redefining Readiness

Grad school will test your confidence in unexpected ways. It will make you question your intelligence, your preparation, and your place. But here's a truth that isn't advertised: **You're not supposed to arrive fully ready.**

You're supposed to learn. To grow. To stumble and rise.

Everyone fails in grad school in some way. Everyone struggles. What matters isn't how perfect your first semester is. What matters is your ability to persevere.

As my mom (another Black woman with a PhD and my #1 role model) reminded me, it's not about how well you do on day one. It's about whether you keep going when things get hard.

That's what a #GRADBOSS does.

Student Voice: Cristina

Cristina started grad school after five years away from academia. At first, she wasn't sure if she could keep up. But she trusted her "why"—her reason for returning. She focused on what mattered: building community, accepting imperfection, and giving herself grace. She graduated with all A's, but more importantly, she left with a new version of success: one rooted in resilience, not pressure.

"Being a #GRADBOSS means being open to mistakes, staying resilient, and lifting others up as you grow." —Cristina

What to Expect (That No One Tells You)

Here's what's *really* true about grad school:
- You'll likely feel behind, even when you're ahead

- Rest will be harder to prioritize, but more important than ever

- Comparison will sneak in, but reflection will keep you grounded

- Your worth is *not* tied to your productivity

- You don't need to do everything—just the right things, consistently

You don't need to figure it all out in your first semester. You just need a system that helps you feel clear, supported, and in control of your time and energy. That's what we'll build together in the chapters ahead.

How to Approach Grad School as a #GRADBOSS

Being a #GRADBOSS isn't about being the most accomplished. It's about being aligned with your goals and values, week by week.

Here's what that might look like:

- You don't wait until the night before to start assignments

- You read *before* class, not just after

- You know how to plan a week based on your energy and deadlines

- You ask for help early

- You protect your rest like it's part of your curriculum (because it is)

And most importantly...You give yourself permission to *learn* grad school, not just survive it.

#GRADBOSS Reflection

- What are you most excited about in grad school?

- What part of this journey feels the most uncertain or overwhelming right now?

- Think about a moment in your life when you struggled and came out stronger. What helped you grow through it?

- What would perseverance look like for you *this* semester?

Chapter Two

Academic Identity, Impostor Syndrome & Belonging

G rad school can challenge everything you thought you knew about yourself.

This chapter helps you rewrite your internal story and learn how to thrive... even when you feel like an outsider.

Who Are You Here?

Grad school isn't just a place. It's a pressure cooker for identity. You step into this new world with all the labels you've collected over the years: smart, driven, quiet, first-gen, overachiever, shy, confident, curious, anxious, successful. Then the classes start. You read articles where you don't recognize half the words. You attend seminars where everyone seems to know more than you. You watch peers speak fluently about their research while you're still trying to remember where the bathroom is in your building.

And suddenly, you're asking yourself questions you've never asked before:

- *Do I really belong here?*

- *Am I smart enough?*

- *What if they made a mistake accepting me?*

- *Who am I in this space?*

These are normal questions. But if you don't address them, they can become identity-defining.

The Impostor Syndrome Spiral

Impostor syndrome isn't about whether you *are* capable. It's about whether you *feel* capable. And in grad school, those feelings are fragile.

You might think impostor syndrome shows up as dramatic self-doubt or public panic. But it's often quieter than that. It sounds like:

- "I should've finished that faster."

- "I probably got lucky on that paper."

- "Everyone else already knows this."

- "Once they see how little I know, it's over."

Impostor syndrome tricks you into shrinking. Into working twice as hard to "catch up." Into hiding your questions or pretending you're okay. It turns growth into performance and belonging into comparison.

But those thoughts and feelings are not the truth. Here's the FACTUAL truth: **You were admitted for a reason. You are not a mistake. You belong.**

Student Voice: Addie

Addie remembers that internal voice, too. As an incoming psychology graduate student, she is beginning her graduate degree with a strong foundation, but impostor syndrome still finds its way in.

"I had to keep reminding myself: You were admitted into the program. You're not supposed to be an expert—you fully belong here."

Before grad school even started, Addi prepared herself by consuming content that made her feel grounded, like The Academic Society's YouTube videos. She built support early and created a mental toolkit she could return to on hard days.

Who Are You Becoming?

One of the biggest shifts in grad school is this: you're not just learning a subject. You're *becoming* a scholar, a researcher, a practitioner. You're stepping into a new academic identity, and that's not a passive process.

It will feel disorienting. You might grieve the confident version of yourself from undergrad. You might feel invisible at first. You might start mimicking others just to keep up.

That's okay.

You're in the messy middle of becoming.

The goal isn't to have your identity figured out on day one. The goal is to stay connected to yourself while your environment changes.

My Story: The Seminar That Shook Me

I remember sitting in a math class during my PhD program, completely lost. Everyone else in the room seemed to be tracking the lecture, asking deep, theoretical questions, nodding along.

And I was just... frozen. I had no idea what was going on.

I remember thinking: *"What if they realize I don't belong here?"*

That feeling—of not knowing, of being behind, of fearing discovery—wasn't new. I had always been a lazy high achiever growing up. I was the one who could do the bare minimum, pay attention in class, and excel. But in grad school, surrounded by people who were just as brilliant and even more ambitious than me, I started questioning my worth in ways I never had before.

The funny thing is, I had *evidence* of my ability: I had passed my exams, earned my place, and done the work. But impostor syndrome made me ignore all that. It made me focus only on what I *didn't* know.

And once I started talking to my classmates, I realized *they all felt the same way.* We were all trying to perform belonging when we already belonged.

High Achievers Are Especially Vulnerable

Impostor syndrome hits hard in grad school, but it hits *hardest* for high achievers. Here's why:

- **Perfectionism** – You hold yourself to such high standards that "good" often feels like "not enough." Grad school forces you to learn in public, make mistakes, and submit imperfect work, so it feels like constant failure, even when it's not.

- **Comparison** – You were probably the standout in under-grad. Now, you're surrounded by other standouts. If you're not careful, you'll start measuring your worth against some-one else's highlight reel.

- **Fear of Failure** – High achievers often equate mistakes with weakness. But in grad school, failure is part of the process. If you don't normalize it, you'll see every setback as confirma-tion that you don't belong.

How to Reclaim Your Academic Identity

Here are some small but powerful ways to stay grounded in who you are:

- **Write a "Why I'm Here" list.** Jot down 3–5 reasons you chose grad school. Refer back when doubt creeps in.

- **Define success on your terms.** Your identity isn't your GPA. It's how you show up. How you rest. How you grow.

- **Find your safe spaces.** Whether it's a peer group, mentor, or the #GRADBOSS community—find people you can be real with.

- **Notice your inner dialogue.** Start replacing thoughts like *"I should know this already"* with *"I'm learning something new today."*

- **Choose identity over insecurity.** Let your actions reflect who you want to become, not who your doubt says you are.

#GRADBOSS Reflection

- When do you feel most like yourself in academic spaces?

- What messages have you internalized about what it means to be "successful" in grad school?

- What's one way you can define or protect your identity this semester?

- If impostor syndrome shows up this week, what would you want a trusted friend to remind you of?

Chapter Three

Know Yourself to Lead Yourself

*D*iscover how your personality, productivity style, and values influence how you navigate school, stress, and success.

Self-Awareness is a Strategy

Grad school asks a lot of you. Every day, you're expected to learn quickly, make decisions, manage your time, lead research projects, speak up in class, and somehow still take care of yourself outside of school. But here's what most programs don't tell you:

You can't lead your academic life well if you don't understand *yourself.*

In the workplace, we often talk about emotional intelligence or leadership styles. In business, we talk about brand identity and audience alignment. But in grad school? We're often told to just keep our heads down and get the work done, without ever asking ourselves:

- *How do I learn best?*

- *What overwhelms me and why?*

- *What values do I want to protect during this degree?*

- *When am I most focused and most depleted?*

- *What helps me come back to myself when things get hard?*

Self-awareness isn't fluffy. It's foundational. The more you understand your energy patterns, your strengths, your blind spots, and your goals, the more equipped you'll be to navigate grad school *on your terms.*

Why Self-Knowledge Matters in Grad School

Self-awareness is more than a personal development buzzword—it's a survival strategy for grad school. When you understand how you operate, what you value, and how you respond to pressure, you can build a grad school experience that supports your growth instead of draining it.

Knowing yourself can help you:

- Manage your time without mimicking someone else's routine

  - **The harm of mimicry:** In grad school, it's easy to assume everyone else has it figured out. You might try to copy your labmate's schedule or follow a classmate's study routine exactly, only to end up exhausted and behind. What works for one person might completely drain another.

- **Why this matters:** When you build your schedule around *your* energy patterns and responsibilities, you can work more effectively and recover faster. You stop wasting time on routines that aren't designed for your brain, your body, or your life.

- Say no to things that don't align with your goals

  - **The harm of overcommitting:** Without clarity on what you value, you might say yes to every opportunity, every committee, every collaboration, every volunteer request. Soon, you're spread thin, doing work that doesn't move you forward.

  - **Why this matters:** Self-knowledge gives you a filter. When you're clear on your goals, you can say no with confidence and yes with intention. This protects your time, your focus, and your long-term vision.

- Choose the right advisor, committee, or research topic

  - **The harm of defaulting:** Choosing an advisor or topic based on prestige—or because someone else told you to—is risky. If their values, communication style, or expectations don't align with yours, the relationship can become a source of constant stress and self-doubt.

  - **Why this matters:** When you know your communication needs, work habits, and research interests, you can choose advisors and projects that energize and support you. The result? A more collaborative, less adversarial grad school experience.

- Recognize burnout *before* you spiral

  - **The harm of ignoring early signs:** Without self-awareness, you might push through exhaustion, numb out with overwork, or normalize constant anxiety. Burnout doesn't usually arrive all at once—it creeps in when you ignore what your mind and body are trying to tell you.

  - **Why this matters:** When you know your warning signs—irritability, brain fog, procrastination, fatigue—you can intervene early. You learn to build rest into your routine *before* you crash. And that means you stay in the game longer and with more clarity.

- Lead projects with confidence

  - **The harm of second-guessing:** If you're unclear on how you lead or teach, you may shrink in collaborative settings. You might struggle to make decisions, over-explain yourself, or defer to others even when you have a strong vision.

  - **Why this matters:** Knowing your leadership style (directive, collaborative, detail-oriented, big picture) helps you own your role. You can delegate, communicate, and contribute without apologizing for who you are, and that confidence creates trust.

- Set boundaries that protect your peace

- **The harm of no boundaries:** Without clear boundaries, grad school will eat up your nights, weekends, and self-worth. You may find yourself answering emails at midnight, saying yes when you want to say no, or neglecting your basic needs in the name of being "productive."

- **Why this matters:** Boundaries are how you protect your energy. When you know your limits and what you need to function well, you can set structure around your time and preserve your sense of self inside and outside of academia.

- Make academic decisions rooted in clarity, not comparison

  - **The harm of comparison-based choices:** When you're unclear about your own priorities, you might make decisions based on what your peers are doing—what they're publishing, how fast they're moving, what internships they're landing. That leads to regret, not fulfillment.

  - **Why this matters:** When you know your path, you can trust it, even if it looks different from others'. Your goals become your compass, not someone else's progress. And that's what keeps you grounded during a degree that's full of distractions.

In short, the better you know yourself, the easier it is to build a grad school experience that works *for you*.

Student Story: Lynn

Lynn's journey into grad school didn't follow the traditional route. He returned to school after years in the workforce, juggling a full-time job and a full graduate course load.

Rather than mimic his younger classmates' study routines, Lynn leaned into what *he* knew worked. He chunked his assignments. He avoided wasting hours on ineffective strategies. And he set boundaries around his time and energy.

"You don't want to be sitting on the computer for four hours. Work smarter, not harder." —Lynn

Lynn's self-awareness as an adult learner helped him thrive, not despite his different path, but because of it.

Productivity Style: There's No One Right Way

Some grad students are planners. Some are sprint-and-recover types. Some thrive in silence. Others need background noise. Some work best in the early morning. Others come alive at night.

There is no one-size-fits-all productivity routine. But there *is* a right way for *you*. Here are a few questions to help you uncover your personal work style:

- When do you feel most focused during the day?

- What kind of environment helps you get started quickly?

- What derails your focus most often?

- Do you need structure (or freedom) to feel productive?

- Do you prefer one long stretch of deep work or several short bursts?

Try tracking your energy for a week. Notice when your brain is sharpest. When your motivation dips. When rest feels most nourishing. That's data you can build your schedule around.

What Are Your Core Values?

Your values shape how you experience grad school, even if you're not always aware of them.

If you value community but isolate yourself to keep up with deadlines, you'll feel misaligned. If you value integrity but say yes to work you resent, you'll feel burned out. If you value freedom but don't build it into your schedule, you'll feel trapped.

Take a moment and ask yourself:

- What do I care most about during this season of life?

- What do I want to protect, even while in grad school?

- What type of academic experience feels *right* for me?

- Am I living in alignment with what I say I value?

The goal is not perfection—it's *congruence*. The more aligned your actions are with your values, the more energized and focused you'll feel.

Student Story: Asha

Asha came into grad school with years of work and life experience. She had a family, a career behind her, and a strong sense of who she was. But that didn't mean she avoided burnout.

For a while, she pushed hard, trying to keep up, trying to perform. Until she realized: her energy wasn't infinite. And her identity wasn't defined by how many hours she could grind.

"Being a #GRADBOSS is really about self-care... being able to say, I can choose to rest or to work—and both are okay." —Asha

Now, Asha builds her schedule around intention. She's still doing the work, but without losing herself in the process.

#GRADBOSS Tips: Lead Yourself Well

Here are three ways to put self-knowledge into practice this week:

1. Build Your Ideal Week Sketch out a week based on your natural energy patterns, not what you *think* it should look like. Protect your peak focus times. Schedule rest *on purpose.*

2. Create a Values Filter List your top 3 values this semester. When an opportunity or decision comes up, ask: *Does this align with what I said matters?*

3. Know Your Reset Button What helps you come back to yourself when you're overwhelmed? A walk? Music? Journaling? A phone call? Make a list. Use it.

#GRADBOSS Reflection

- When do I feel most energized and most depleted?

- What are three values I want to honor this semester?

- Where in my current routine am I ignoring my needs or patterns?

- What does self-leadership look like for me right now?

Part II: Plan with Purpose

Create systems that reduce overwhelm and work for your life, not just your program.

Chapter Four

Preparing for a New Semester

Your semester starts long before classes begin. We'll walk through mindset prep, reflection, and ritual to set yourself up for a semester of success and ease.

Start Before It Starts

Most grad students wait until the first week of classes to get organized. But the secret to a smooth semester? **It starts *before* the calendar does.**

This doesn't mean you need to build an elaborate study system over the break or dive into writing papers weeks in advance. It just means that *a little reflection, a little prep, and a few small rituals* can completely shift how the semester begins and how it flows.

When you start the semester with intention, you:

- Reduce the chaos of the first week

- Enter your courses with clarity and confidence

- Feel more grounded in your time and energy

- Stop reacting and start leading your grad school experience

The Pre-Semester Reset

Before I figured this out, my semesters always started the same way: Stress. Scrambling. Overwhelm.

The first week felt like a flood of syllabi, login emails, awkward intros, and anxiety. I'd try to get it all sorted while still clinging to the last remnants of my break. I *never* felt ready.

Eventually, I realized I didn't need more motivation.

I needed a *reset*.

Now, I give myself space for a full reset before each semester—a pause, a plan, and a few grounding practices that help me shift from "vacation brain" to "grad boss mode" without panic. This chapter walks you through how to do the same.

Why Preparation Matters (and What Happens If You Skip It)

Grad school has a way of taking over everything. It sneaks into your weekends, eats into your sleep, and convinces you that if you're not constantly working, you're falling behind. That feeling doesn't start mid-semester; it starts when the semester begins in chaos.

When you don't take time to prepare, you're more likely to:

- Miss important deadlines during Week 1

- Underestimate your workload

- Struggle with time management

- Say yes to things that don't align with your goals

- Fall into comparison or panic when others seem more "on top of it" than you

- Burn out by Week 4, not Week 14

And you deserve better than that. You deserve a semester that reflects your goals, honors your energy, and leaves room for joy and rest. That kind of semester doesn't just happen. It's designed *by you*.

Step 1: Reflect on the Last Semester

Before you begin planning for the months ahead, look back. Whether this is your first semester or your fifth, take time to pause and consider what's brought you to this moment.

Ask yourself:

- What went well last semester?

- What drained me the most?

- Where did I feel most confident—and most overwhelmed?

- What routines or habits helped me thrive?

- What do I want to do differently this time?

This is not about judgment. It's about gathering data from your own life. Let your experience guide your strategy.

Even if this is your very first semester, you can still reflect. Consider what kind of student you've been in the past and how grad school might require something different from you.

Write it down. Say it out loud. Talk it through with a peer. This is your data. Let it guide you forward.

Step 2: Choose Your Anchor Goals

Rather than starting the semester with a list of 17 different goals (which will likely lead to guilt and burnout), choose 1–3 **anchor goals**. These are goals that:

- Keep you focused when things get busy

- Support your academic AND personal growth

- Are rooted in intention, not pressure

Examples:

- Submit my first conference abstract

- Start each week with a 30-minute planning session

- Go to bed before midnight 4 nights a week

- Complete my lab notebook weekly

- Connect with my advisor at least once a month

Anchor goals should feel doable, grounding, and relevant to *your* life. If they feel heavy, simplify.

Step 3: Design Your Rituals

One of the biggest shocks in grad school is the sudden shift in structure (or lack of it). Especially if your program includes research, independent study, or unstructured time, you might find yourself waking up without a clear plan for the day.

That's why it helps to gently begin your semester rhythm before it officially begins.

Start by practicing your ideal wake-up and work times. If you know you'll have morning classes or afternoon meetings, begin shifting your sleep schedule now. Choose a consistent time to start reading or studying each day, even if it's just for 30 minutes. You're not trying to get ahead. You're just training your body and brain to focus when you need it most.

Think of it like stretching before a long run. It prevents injury and gives you the endurance to keep going. Small rituals make a big difference in how you start, sustain, and end your semester. Here are a few rituals to consider:

Pre-Semester Rituals:

- Do a deep clean of your workspace

- Set up your calendar or planner

- Update your grad school Notion, Trello, or folder system

- Write a short welcome note to yourself for the new semester

Weekly Rituals:

- Monday morning planning session

- Sunday night reset: review deadlines, prep meals, pick outfits

- Midweek check-in: "What's working? What needs to shift?"

End-of-Semester Rituals:

- Write down your proudest moments (big or small)

- List 3 things you learned about yourself

- Celebrate—even if it's just a solo dance party or fancy coffee

Rituals aren't just about productivity. They're about *ownership*. About turning your semester into a rhythm instead of a race.

Student Voice: Cristina

Cristina always returned to one thing during her program: her "why."

"I came to grad school with purpose. When things got hard, I went back to that."

Before every semester, Cristina would revisit her long-term goals and remind herself what success meant *to her*, not just what the program expected.

That helped her stay focused, even when impostor syndrome or burnout tried to pull her off course.

Step 4: Clarify Your Non-Negotiables

Your non-negotiables are the things that keep you well. They're often the first things to disappear during busy seasons, but they're also the things that help you recover fastest when grad school gets tough.

For me, it was a bedtime routine, solo coffee dates, and calling my mom once a week. When I stopped doing those things, I felt more anxious and disconnected. When I protected them, I felt grounded.

What are yours?

It could be daily movement, journaling, a weekly hangout with a friend, or attending a worship service. Whatever helps you feel like yourself—*name it, and then schedule it.* Don't wait until things calm down. Guard your well-being from the start.

Step 5: Create a Soft Start Plan

Your first week of the semester doesn't need to be perfect, but it *should* be intentional. This is your opportunity to reduce decision fatigue, simplify your routines, and remove as much chaos as possible from those opening days.

Here are a few soft start steps you can take in the week or two before classes begin:

- Set up your planner or digital calendar

- Review any available syllabi and add key dates

- Figure out how long it takes to get to campus at peak times

- Clean and refresh your workspace

- Test your logins and platforms (Zoom, Canvas, email)

- Set up a simple meal plan for Week 1

- Choose your outfits or create a "first week capsule wardrobe"

- Prepare a go-to response for introducing yourself in class or lab meetings

None of these tasks are urgent, but they're deeply helpful. The less you have to figure out on the fly, the more presence and confidence you'll bring to your first week.

#GRADBOSS Step: Define What Success Looks Like

Here's where most grad students go wrong: they define success as *doing everything perfectly.*

But a #GRADBOSS defines success as *progress with purpose.* As showing up consistently, not flawlessly. As honoring your energy while protecting your momentum.

Before the semester begins, write down:

- One personal goal

- One academic goal

- One thing you want to feel more of (confidence, calm, connection, etc.)

Let those be your North Star. If you only did *those three things*, would the semester still feel meaningful? If the answer is yes—you're already winning.

Student Voice: Briana

When I interviewed Briana, a PhD student in disease ecology, she told me that part of preparing for a new semester is being open to growth—even the kind you can't predict.

"You may do things you never realized you're capable of doing. Make space for that."

That's what this chapter is about. Creating space, not for perfection, but for possibility. For flexibility. For steady, self-led progress.

Your Semester, Your Way

Grad school isn't just about passing classes and completing research. It's about learning how to live well under pressure. And the truth is, semesters don't spiral because we're lazy. They spiral because we're unprepared.

This is your reminder that you can begin gently. You can choose calm. You can set yourself up to succeed, not by working more, but by starting with intention.

You'll find additional planning tools, reflection pages, and a weekly schedule template in the **Resources & Reflections** section at the back of this book. If you want a soft place to land each semester, those tools are there to guide you. Your semester doesn't have to start in chaos. It can start with clarity.

Your Pre-Semester Reset Ritual

Set aside one afternoon or evening before the semester begins to walk yourself through this ritual:

1. Reflect on the past semester

2. Write your three anchor goals

3. Identify your non-negotiables and schedule them

4. Set up your calendar, workspace, and logins

5. Plan your first week of meals and movement

6. Choose a calming or energizing ritual to start your mornings

7. Write a short note to yourself: "This semester, I choose..."

You can even repeat this ritual before every semester (or at the start of each month) as a way to realign.

Chapter Five

Creating a Productive Weekly Schedule

Time management is more than just getting stuff done; it's about building a life you actually want to live. Let's design your ideal week.

Most grad students don't have a time management problem.

They have a *time awareness* problem.

You're doing so much (reading, teaching, researching, writing, attending class, trying to be a human), but your schedule doesn't reflect any of it clearly. You're busy all day and somehow still behind. You collapse into bed at midnight, unsure of what you actually accomplished.

That's where a weekly schedule comes in. Not as a rigid plan, but as a flexible framework. A weekly schedule gives you clarity. It helps you prioritize what matters, reclaim your energy, and move through your semester with intention instead of anxiety.

Why You Need a Weekly Plan (Even If You Hate Routines)

Some people *love* planners. (Me!) They color-code every task and sync every calendar. But even if that's not your vibe, creating a weekly rhythm can be one of the most supportive things you do in grad school. Because without a plan, here's what tends to happen:

- You spend more time *deciding* what to do than doing it

- Small tasks eat up your whole day, leaving no time for big ones

- You procrastinate on long-term projects because they don't have built-in deadlines

- You overwork during the week and burn out on the weekends

- You constantly feel behind, even when you're keeping up

And that can leave you feeling like grad school is running you instead of the other way around.

But when you create a weekly structure (even a loose one), you take back control. You stop reacting and start leading.

Step 1: Know Your Time Budget

You wouldn't build a financial budget without knowing your income. The same goes for time.

Start by mapping out your *non-negotiables* for the week:

- Classes and labs

- Teaching or grading responsibilities

- Work or assistantship hours

- Commutes

- Meals and sleep

- Weekly commitments (religious services, caregiving, etc.)

Now count what's left. This is your actual *available time*, and it's probably less than you think.

That's okay. This awareness will help you stop overcommitting and *start protecting* the time you have.

Step 2: Design Your Ideal Week

Once you know what time is available, you can begin building your weekly template.

I recommend blocking out your schedule in four main categories:

1. Academic Time – Reading, writing, studying, research, coursework

2. Admin Time – Emails, scheduling, errands, TA prep, tech/logistical tasks

3. Rest & Reset – Meals, breaks, walks, naps, screen-free time

4. Personal Time – Time with loved ones, hobbies, appointments, joy

Here is an example of a schedule:

(Note the productivity chunks. We will discuss these in detail next.)

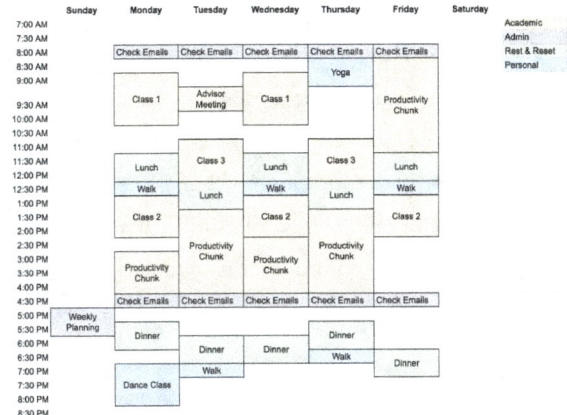

The goal isn't to fill every hour. It's to *assign meaning* to your time before it fills itself.

The Power of Productivity Chunks

Here's a mindset shift that changed everything for me in grad school:

Productivity isn't about checking off a to-do list—it's about showing up for the work when it matters.

That's where *productivity chunks* come in.

A productivity chunk is a focused block of time (anywhere from 2 to 5 hours) set aside for deep, meaningful work. But unlike traditional scheduling methods, you don't fill this block with a rigid list of tasks. You simply label it for what it is: time to be productive.

That's it.

You don't have to decide in advance whether you'll be writing, grading, responding to emails, or prepping for your lab meeting. Instead, you give yourself a flexible window where your only goal is *to be productive with intention.*

Why Productivity Chunks Work

Traditional task lists sound helpful...until you can't stick to them. Something always comes up: an urgent email from your advisor, a surprise TA assignment, a department meeting you didn't plan for. And when you've packed your schedule with a minute-by-minute list of "must-do" tasks, those interruptions feel like failures.

But a productivity chunk gives you flexibility.If your morning goes off the rails, your afternoon productivity chunk is still open.If a last-minute request comes in, you can handle it *without* throwing off your entire week.

The best part? You still get things done, but with way less guilt and way more adaptability.

How to Use Productivity Chunks

Here's how to incorporate them into your weekly schedule:

1. **Identify your focused work windows** – Look for times when your energy is highest and distractions are lowest. These are your prime productivity hours.

2. **Block out 2–5 hour chunks** – Add them to your calendar as "Productivity Chunk", not "Read Ch. 3" or "Write IRB." Let the work flex based on what's most important that day.

3. **Create a running task bank** – Instead of assigning specific tasks to each chunk, keep a list of ongoing priorities (like writing, grading, emails, reading). When the time block begins, choose based on your energy and urgency.

4. **Protect these chunks like meetings** – Don't give them away. Don't multitask them. Don't scroll through them. This is your focused time, and you're allowed to take it seri-

ously.

A #GRADBOSS Reminder:

Productivity chunks aren't about perfection. They're about *presence.*

They give you space to pivot, room to breathe, and permission to change course without feeling like you've failed. Whether you use one productivity chunk a day or one a week, the point is to create a rhythm that honors your capacity while moving your goals forward.

Let your schedule work *with* you—not against you.

#GRADBOSS Tip: Use Theme Days or Time Blocks

Instead of scheduling every minute, consider setting themes for your days or blocks for your focus.

Examples:

- **Monday Mornings**: Class prep + planning the week

- **Tuesday Afternoons**: Research + advisor tasks

- **Wednesdays**: Writing + errands

- **Friday Mornings**: Admin tasks + email cleanup

- **Sunday Nights**: Reset + schedule review

When you know what each part of your day is *for*, you spend less energy deciding, and more energy doing.

Step 3: Plan, But Leave Room for Life

Things will change. Meetings will shift. A paper will take longer than expected. You'll get sick or overwhelmed or need a day to rest.

That's why your weekly schedule should be *adaptive*, not rigid. Leave buffer time between tasks. Plan for catch-up hours. Give yourself full blocks of unstructured time where nothing is scheduled *on purpose.*

Remember: white space on your calendar is not laziness. It's strategy.

Step 4: Make Weekly Planning a Ritual

Your schedule won't serve you if you never look at it. Choose one time each week (Sunday night, Monday morning), or whatever works for you, to sit down and review:

- What's coming up this week?

- What deadlines do I need to work toward?

- What's my biggest priority for each day?

- Where do I need to protect rest?

- What might throw me off—and how can I adjust?

This is how you stay aligned with your goals instead of getting pulled by everyone else's priorities.

Student Voice: Asha

For Asha, a returning grad student with a family and a full life outside of school, scheduling wasn't just about time, it was about energy.

"Being a #GRADBOSS is really about self-care... being able to say, I can choose to rest or to work—and both are okay."

Her weekly schedule included boundaries around sleep, time with her kids, and solo rest time. She built her productivity around her *life*, not the other way around.

Try This: Build Your #GRADBOSS Weekly Schedule

1. Map your fixed commitments

2. Block time for academic work

3. Add in admin and life logistics

4. Schedule your rest + non-negotiables

5. Leave buffer blocks

6. Choose a weekly planning day + stick to it

7. Write a mantra for the week: *"This week, I focus on _____ and protect_____."*

You'll find planning templates in the **Resources & Reflections** section at the back of this book.

Your Time = Your Power

When you treat your time with intention, you treat your *life* with intention. You stop letting grad school consume every hour, and you start creating a rhythm that reflects your real priorities.

You don't need a perfect plan. You just need a flexible one that supports your energy, your goals, and your peace.

That's what it means to be a #GRADBOSS.

Chapter Six

Setting Goals That Actually Guide You

*B*ig goals are great...but weekly goals help you move. This chapter gives you a framework to prioritize without burning out.

Let's get one thing out of the way: you are already ambitious. If you're in grad school, it means you've set big goals, pursued them relentlessly, and made it through all the gatekeeping to get here.

But here's the hard part that no one warns you about: The same ambition that got you into grad school can make it *really hard* to navigate once you're in it.

That's because grad school isn't a clear path. It's a long, winding trail with detours, obstacles, and shifting expectations. You might start with one goal and find yourself in an entirely different research direction. You might be so overwhelmed with day-to-day tasks that you forget why you're doing any of it in the first place.

That's why you need to rethink what goal-setting looks like in grad school. It's not just about where you want to end up, it's about how to keep moving, even when things get hard.

What Happens When You Don't Set the *Right* Goals

Most grad students are *not* short on goals. In fact, you probably have too many. You want to finish your coursework, publish a paper, ace your qualifying exams, impress your advisor, stay close to your friends, be a supportive partner or parent, get enough sleep, start a business or side project, maybe even take a vacation...

That's not a goals problem. That's a *capacity* problem. When your list is full of unclear, unrealistic, or overly ambitious goals, here's what tends to happen:

- You feel overwhelmed before you even begin

- You don't know what to prioritize on a daily basis

- You procrastinate because the goals feel too big to start

- You don't celebrate progress because you're focused only on the end result

- You burn out from constantly chasing a moving target

And over time, you start wondering: *Am I even doing enough? Am I falling behind?*

The solution? **Smaller, clearer, aligned goals that actually guide your week, not just your year.**

Step 1: Set Goals at the Right Level

There's nothing wrong with long-term goals. In fact, you'll probably have a few floating in your head at all times:

- Finish your dissertation

- Land a great job after graduation

- Get a paper accepted

- Launch a project or program

But if you stop at these high-level outcomes, you'll struggle with focus and follow-through.

That's why we break goals down into **levels:**

1. **Vision-Level Goals:** Big-picture outcomes (e.g., graduate in 5 years, become a faculty member, build a portfolio career, get published)

2. **Semester Goals:** The "big three" you want to focus on this term (e.g., pass qualifying exams, complete a research chapter, present at a conference)

3. **Weekly Goals:** Concrete, doable action items that move you forward (e.g., read 3 articles, draft intro, schedule advisor meeting)

You should revisit your **vision goals** once per semester, your **semester goals** monthly, and your **weekly goals** every 7 days.

Weekly goals are where the real movement happens. Because grad school success is built one week at a time.

Step 2: Focus on Progress, Not Pressure

Every goal you set should do two things:

1. Guide your actions

2. Protect your energy

If your goals only make you feel guilty, they're not doing their job. Here's a quick test for a good weekly goal:

- *Can you clearly identify what "done" looks like?*

- *Can you realistically complete it with the time and energy you have?*

- *Does it connect back to something bigger you care about?*

If the answer is no to any of those, revise it. Make it smaller. More tangible. More meaningful. Here are some examples of aligned weekly goals:

- Finish outline for literature review

- Submit TA schedule preferences

- Send feedback to co-author

- Attend one research seminar

- Take a full day off with no academic tasks

Yes, rest can be a goal, too.

Step 3: Use a Weekly Planning Framework

Here's a simple process I recommend every week (I do this every Sunday night or Monday morning):

The Weekly Planning Framework

1. Review last week

- What did I finish?

- What's still in progress?

- What felt good or hard?

2. Reconnect to your goals

- What am I working toward this semester?

- What small wins can I aim for this week?

3. Choose 3 focus goals These should feel clear, possible, and helpful.

4. Schedule your priorities Look at your calendar. Block time for these goals *first*, before adding other tasks.

5. Leave space At least one free afternoon or block of "catch-up" time.

Student Voice: Briana

Briana learned that her goals weren't just about output. They were about *alignment*.

"I had to ask: Is this task leading me where I want to go? Or is it just keeping me busy?"

She began filtering her to-dos through that lens and let go of the ones that didn't fit.

#GRADBOSS Tip: Use Goal Themes

If you're juggling a lot, try assigning *themes* to each week based on what needs the most attention.

Examples:

- **Week 2:** "Catch-Up and Clean-Up" – focus on small admin tasks and course corrections

- **Week 4:** "Deep Work Sprint" – block time for focused writing or research

- **Week 7:** "Rest + Recharge" – keep goals light and focus on recovery

Let your goals reflect your energy and priorities—not just your deadlines.

Try This: The #GRADBOSS Weekly Goal Planner

At the start of each week:

- Write down one academic goal

- Write down one personal or rest goal

- Write down one "supportive" goal (e.g., connect with a mentor, prep for a meeting, organize files)

- Schedule your focus blocks for the week

- Circle one day when you'll do *no schoolwork*

You'll find a printable version of this planner in the **Resources & Reflections** section at the back of this book.

Progress Is the Point

In grad school, the work is never truly "done." There's always another paper to revise, another reading to skim, another dataset to clean. That's why success can't be defined by checking every box.

Instead, define your success by whether you're moving in the direction you want to go and whether your goals are helping you *live* that journey, not just survive it.

Big dreams matter. But consistent, aligned action is what turns them into reality.

Part III: Get Stuff Done (Without Losing Yourself)

Strategies for productivity, motivation, and staying focused when things get hard.

Chapter Seven

The Productivity Accelerator Method

The three-part method that helps grad students get out of the procrastination cycle and back into momentum. (Spoiler: it's not just about discipline.)

If you've ever sat at your desk for three hours with a full to-do list and somehow accomplished nothing... you're not alone.

If you've opened your laptop, stared at a blank screen, and then found yourself doom-scrolling Twitter (or X) or deep in a "How to Study in Grad School" YouTube rabbit hole... still not alone.

Grad school is full of smart, ambitious people who suddenly find it *really hard to get things done*. And the usual advice—just focus more, try harder, eliminate distractions—rarely works.

That's why I created the **Productivity Accelerator Method**: a three-part framework to help you move through procrastination with compassion and clarity, and actually *get back to work* when your brain wants to shut down.

The Myth of Academic Discipline

There's this unspoken assumption in grad school that if you really cared, you'd be productive. That if you were smart enough, committed enough, or passionate enough, you'd be working 12-hour days in a flurry of papers and breakthroughs.

But that's not how productivity works, especially for high-achievers dealing with overwhelm, perfectionism, or impostor syndrome.

Productivity isn't about *doing more.* It's about doing the *right things* at the right time, with the right mindset and structure to support you. And that's exactly what this method is designed to help you do.

Why Grad Students Get Stuck

Before we jump into the solution, let's name the problem. Grad students tend to get stuck in a specific type of productivity cycle:

- You have a big task (write paper, study, prep for meeting)

- You feel overwhelmed, unsure, or unmotivated

- You procrastinate, distract yourself, or avoid the task

- Guilt kicks in

- The task feels even heavier

- Repeat

The longer you stay in this cycle, the harder it feels to restart. And what begins as a "quick break" turns into days (or weeks) of avoidance.

The Productivity Accelerator Method breaks this cycle in three steps.

Step 1: Zoom Out

When you're stuck, your brain gets hyper-focused on how hard everything feels. So the first step is to *zoom out* and take inventory.

Ask yourself:

- What's the actual task I'm avoiding?

- Why does it feel hard right now?

- Is it too big, too vague, or too boring?

- Am I tired, hungry, anxious, or distracted?

This isn't just about self-awareness, it's about *intervention*. When you understand the block, you can address it directly.

If the task feels too big → break it downIf it feels too boring → pair it with music or a cozy setting If you're overwhelmed → talk it out with a friend or advisor If you're mentally exhausted → give yourself permission to rest first

Productivity without awareness is just noise. Awareness turns chaos into clarity.

Step 2: Anchor Your Focus

Once you've identified what's going on, it's time to ground your attention with a simple question:

What's the next thing I can do that would move this forward (even just a little)?

Not "what's the perfect next step." Not "what should I do if I had all day." Just *the next, tiny, doable thing*.

Examples:

- Open the article and read the abstract

- Write one messy paragraph

- Open your project doc and title it

- Create the citation list

- Draft a bullet-point outline

By giving your brain something concrete and immediate, you bypass the fear and resistance that comes with thinking too far ahead.

This is about momentum, not mastery.

Step 3: Choose Your Container

Once you know what you're doing, the final step is choosing *how* you'll do it and for how long.

That means creating a focused **container** for your work. Something that signals: "I'm in it now."

Your container could be:

- A **time block** (e.g., work for 25 minutes, then rest for 5)

- A **coworking session** (virtual or in-person)

- A **location shift** (head to a new space to signal a new focus)

- A **playlist or timer** (create a productivity ritual with sound or scent)

- A **body cue** (light a candle, put your hair in a bun, change into a "work hoodie")

The container isn't about forcing productivity. It's about creating the conditions for focus to happen more naturally.

Student Voice: Asya

Asya, who rediscovered her academic rhythm after burnout, told me she now creates containers for everything.

"I used to try to push through overwhelm. Now, I make a cozy space, set a time, and tell myself: you only have to start."

Her advice to others? *Start small, but start with care.*

Bonus: Use the Momentum Multiplier

When you complete a productivity chunk (see Chapter 5), end with intention:

1. **Celebrate** what you got done

2. **Plan the next step** so Future You doesn't have to guess

3. **Reset your space** so your next session feels like a fresh start

This keeps the momentum flowing instead of stopping abruptly.

Try This: The Productivity Accelerator Reset

When you're stuck, walk yourself through these steps:

Zoom Out: What's hard right now? What's the task *really* asking of me?

Anchor Your Focus: What's the next small, clear action I can take?

Choose Your Container: What environment or time frame will support me?

Then start. Just for 10 minutes. That's all.

Often, you'll go longer than that. But the win is starting.

Progress Is a Practice

You don't have to be a productivity machine to succeed in grad school.

You just need tools that support *who you are*, not who academia expects you to be.

The Productivity Accelerator Method isn't about perfect output. It's about progress that honors your humanity. It's a way to return to your work with less shame, more strategy, and a little bit of softness.

You can restart. As many times as you need to. You can get things done *without* burning out. You can lead your work instead of letting it control you.

That's what this method makes possible.

Chapter Eight

Productivity With Unstructured Time

What do you do when no one is telling you what to do? Here's how to create your own structure and stay on track—especially in research years.

One of the most disorienting parts of grad school is this: **No one is watching your every move.**

Unlike undergrad, or even the early semesters of your graduate program, there comes a point when there's *no one* checking if you did the reading, no quiz to confirm you understood the seminar, no formal assignment to prove you made progress on your research this week.

It's just you.

You and your research. You and your dissertation. You and the vast, unstructured timeline that suddenly makes productivity feel… optional and overwhelming all at once.

If you've ever thought:

- "I had all day and still didn't get anything done."

- "I know what I need to do… but I just can't get started."

- "I feel so guilty for wasting time."

This chapter is for you.

The Structure-Free Spiral

Many grad students hit a wall when coursework ends and the research phase begins. Suddenly, the built-in structure disappears:

- No fixed class schedule

- No weekly homework deadlines

- No advisor meetings unless *you* schedule them

And while that freedom might sound amazing at first (hello, sleeping in and midday strolls), it can quickly turn into a spiral:

- You sleep in later than intended

- You procrastinate because there's "always tomorrow"

- You lose track of time

- You feel guilty for being unproductive

- You avoid work to avoid the guilt

- You feel even *less* motivated

This is why creating your own structure is one of the most essential skills of grad school success.

And the best part? It doesn't have to be rigid, intense, or over-whelming. You can build flexible systems that support *you*, your brain, your body, your work style, and your goals.

Step 1: Name Your Priorities

When everything feels vague, your first job is to bring clarity to what actually matters.

Ask yourself:

- What are the top 1–2 outcomes I want to make progress on this month?

- What weekly action(s) will move those forward?

- What tasks tend to get neglected that are still important?

Make a short list. Keep it visible. This is your compass when time feels slippery.

Remember: you don't need a 40-item to-do list. You need 2–3 *directional priorities* that help you choose your next best action.

Step 2: Create a Weekly Skeleton

Your schedule may be unstructured but that doesn't mean it should be empty. Use a blank weekly calendar and build your "skeleton":

- Add *fixed appointments* (teaching, meetings, classes)

- Block *Productivity Chunks* (see Chapter 5) for deep work

- Schedule 1–2 *flex blocks* for catch-up or rest

- Add *weekly rituals* like planning, check-ins, or advisor prep

- Leave space for unstructured, restorative time

You don't have to fill every hour. Just create *enough structure* that your day has shape and your priorities have a place to land.

This is what keeps you grounded when deadlines are months (or years) away.

Step 3: Time Anchor Your Day

Without classes or external cues, time can feel fuzzy. That's why it helps to anchor your day with *time markers* that tell your brain, "This is work time" or "This is rest." Here are a few examples:

- **Morning Anchor** – A consistent start-time or ritual that eases you into the day (e.g., make tea, review your goals, stretch, read for 20 minutes)

- **Midday Anchor** – A lunch break, a walk, or a phone call that separates work sessions

- **Evening Anchor** – A shutdown ritual that helps you transition out of "grad student mode" (e.g., close your laptop, light a candle, change clothes, text a friend)

These time anchors provide structure without pressure. They help your brain shift gears and protect your boundaries between work and rest.

#GRADBOSS Tip: Use Gentle Deadlines

One of the best tools I've used (and taught my students to use) is the **gentle deadline.**

Here's how it works:

- Choose a small, specific task

- Set a soft deadline (e.g., "I'll finish this draft by Friday at 3pm")

- Add a layer of support (co-working session, accountability text, calendar reminder)

- If you miss it, *no shame.* Just review what got in the way and adjust your next deadline

Gentle deadlines give your week direction without the shame spiral of missed goals.

Step 4: Track Your Progress *Backwards*

Instead of only measuring success by what you *planned* to do, try tracking what you *actually* did.

At the end of each day or week, ask:

- What did I work on today?

- What moved forward, even slightly?

- What did I learn, notice, or improve?

This reverse-tracking approach helps you build confidence and momentum, even when you didn't hit every target.

Plus, it helps you spot patterns: what time of day you're most focused, which tasks you avoid, how long certain projects actually take.

Unstructured Doesn't Mean Unguided

Unstructured time is one of the greatest challenges *and* greatest privileges of grad school. It's where you learn to lead yourself, make decisions independently, and trust your own rhythms. But that doesn't mean you have to do it alone or figure it out from scratch.

You can build your own structure. You can anchor your day with intention. You can move through long research phases with clarity and grace.

You're not lazy. You just need rhythm. And you're more capable than you think.

Chapter Nine

Working from Home Without Losing Focus

*F*rom designated work zones to distraction-busting routines, these tips help you stay productive wherever you are.

There's something both magical and terrifying about working from home.

On the one hand, you can wear cozy clothes, light a candle, and work from your favorite corner of the couch. On the other hand, that same couch might be whispering, "Nap instead?" before you've even opened your laptop.

Working from home can be deeply productive *or* deeply distracting. The difference? Intention.

Whether you're taking a remote course, conducting research, writing your thesis, or just working from home between meetings, this chapter will help you build an environment that invites focus without sacrificing comfort or joy.

The Home-Based Productivity Trap

Here's what often happens:

- You wake up without a clear plan

- You tell yourself you'll "ease into the day"

- Suddenly it's 2:00 p.m. and all you've done is check email, do laundry, and scroll

- You feel guilty for not being productive, so you work late to compensate

- The cycle repeats

This doesn't mean you're bad at working from home. It just means you haven't set up systems to support you yet.

Let's fix that.

Step 1: Choose a Focus Zone (Even If It's Small)

You don't need a full home office. But you do need a *space* that tells your brain, "This is where focus happens."

This might be:

- A desk in the corner of your bedroom

- A seat at your kitchen table with a specific notebook and mug

- A certain chair with your laptop, headphones, and blanket nearby

- A portable setup you take to different rooms, but always use the same way

The key is consistency.

Even if you live with roommates, family, or kids, you can still carve out a work zone that feels like *yours.* That small sense of separation between "work mode" and "rest mode" matters.

Step 2: Set Your Signal Rituals

Signal rituals are small, repeatable actions that let your brain know that it's time to work now. These rituals don't have to be elaborate. Just consistent. For example:

- Light a specific candle

- Put on headphones and your "focus" playlist

- Open your planner and write your top 3 tasks

- Change into a work hoodie or sweater

- Make tea in your favorite mug

These signals tell your body and mind: "We're transitioning into focused energy now."

Likewise, you can create a shutdown ritual for the end of your day:

- Close your laptop

- Write a quick progress note or tomorrow's to-do list

- Turn off your workspace light

- Take a walk or change into comfy clothes

These boundaries help you shift back into rest, so you're not "always working" just because your work is nearby.

Step 3: Minimize Multitasking (And Overwhelm)

The home environment often makes multitasking feel unavoidable:

- You open a research article, then remember you need to start laundry

- You answer an email, then check your group chat, then go make lunch

- You start reading... then fall down a social media rabbit hole

The fix? Reduce distractions.

Here's how:

- Keep your phone in a separate room or face down on do-not-disturb

- Use browser extensions like **FocusMode** or **StayFocusd** to limit distractions

- Schedule home tasks for *before or after* work blocks, not during

- Use the **Pomodoro method** (25 minutes on, 5 minutes off or 45 minutes on, 10 minutes off for deeper work) to stay on track

- Keep only one tab open if you're doing deep reading or

writing

And remember: *you don't need to eliminate every distraction.* You just need enough structure to stay in flow when it matters.

Step 4: Time-Block With Grace

Working from home gives you flexibility, but *too* much flexibility can lead to drift. Instead of filling your entire day with tasks, try **Time-Blocking Lite**:

- Block off **1–2 Productivity Chunks** (see Chapter 5)

- Leave room for spontaneity or rest

- Include breaks *on purpose* so you don't burn out

- Give each block a theme (writing, reading, grading, admin)

Example:

- 9–11:30am → Research Writing

- 12–1pm → Lunch + Break

- 1–2pm → Emails + Admin

- 2–4pm → Read Articles + Notetaking

- 4–5pm → Soft Stop + Shutdown Ritual

Step 5: Honor Your Energy

Working from home gives you the rare ability to work in alignment with your natural energy cycles. Use it.

Ask yourself:
- When do I feel most clear and focused? (Morning, afternoon, evening?)

- When do I tend to hit a wall or need rest?

- What foods, movement, or routines give me energy?

Then, design your schedule to match.

You're not lazy for taking a mid-afternoon walk. You're not behind because you need more sleep. You're listening to your body, and that's what #GRADBOSSes do.

Your Home, Your Rules

Here's what working from home really teaches you:
- You don't need constant pressure to be productive

- You can design an environment that supports your goals

- You can focus and rest in a way that feels good, not forced

You're not trying to replicate a library or a lab. You're creating a cozy, clear, intentional space for your academic work (and your well-being) to thrive side by side. You're allowed to feel at home in both.

Part IV: Real Life in Grad School

Relationships, rest, and redefining what balance really means.

Chapter Ten

Work-Life-Self-Care Integration

L *et's drop the idea of "balance" and instead explore how to shift your energy based on what matters most.*

You've probably heard it a hundred times: "Grad school is all about work-life balance."

But let's be honest... balance? That's a lot of pressure. The word "balance" suggests that you're supposed to hold everything (your classes, your research, your relationships, your well-being) in perfect harmony at all times. And if you drop a ball? You've failed.

But *balance* isn't always realistic. Especially in grad school, where demands can change week to week (and sometimes hour to hour). That's why this chapter offers something better: **Integration.**

Integration Over Balance

Work-life-self-care integration is about:

- Understanding your current capacity

- Adjusting your energy accordingly

- Staying rooted in what matters most, even when things get messy

Instead of asking, "How do I keep everything perfectly balanced?" We ask, "What needs more of me right now and what can wait?"

Integration honors the ebb and flow of grad school life. It lets you make intentional choices instead of chasing impossible perfection.

The 4-Bucket Method

This is one of the most helpful tools I've used (and taught) to manage competing priorities without burning out. It works like this:

Bucket 1: Work

Your grad school tasks like classes, research, grading, teaching, writing

Bucket 2: Life

Errands, finances, household responsibilities, appointments, commuting

Bucket 3: Relationships

Time with family, friends, partners, mentors, and peers

Bucket 4: Self-Care

Sleep, rest, joy, movement, nourishment, therapy, hobbies, journaling

Each week, you do a quick pulse check:

- Which bucket is overflowing?

- Which one is running dry?

- Which one needs my attention most right now?

Then, you plan your week with intention—not to *do everything*, but to *nurture what's most in need.*

Some weeks, your "Work" bucket needs the most energy (dissertation deadline, midterms). Other times, your "Self-Care" bucket is on empty and needs to come first. That's not imbalance. That's *wise management of your energy.*

Step 1: Take Inventory

Grab a notebook, tablet, or Google doc and for each bucket, ask:

- What's filling this bucket right now?

- What's draining it?

- What do I need more of?

This check-in takes five minutes but it can shift your entire week.

Step 2: Protect Your Anchor Activities

Anchor activities are the small things that keep you steady. You may have already identified some in Chapter 4 when we talked about non-negotiables.

Here's the reminder: Protect them. Even in busy seasons. Especially in busy seasons.

You don't need 10 self-care rituals a day. You need 1–2 that *work*, and that you'll actually do.

Examples:

- A 10-minute walk between work sessions

- Journaling before bed

- A midweek phone call with someone who makes you laugh

- A Saturday morning with no emails or work talk

These are the small acts that remind you: **I am a whole person, not just a grad student.**

Step 3: Create Integration Routines

Let's shift from "balance" to *blending*.

Try these small shifts:

- Listen to an academic podcast while doing chores

- Review flashcards during your commute

- Read for fun at lunch to break up academic reading

- Meal prep while chatting with a friend

- Set office hours for yourself, even when working from home

Integration is about combining, aligning, and adjusting your tasks to serve both your goals and your well-being.

#GRADBOSS Tip: Track Your Energy

If you've ever ended the week thinking, "Where did all my time go?"—try tracking your energy instead of your hours.

Each evening, jot down:

- What gave me energy today?

- What drained me?

- What surprised me?

After a week, review your patterns. This will help you plan future weeks around your *real* capacity, not just your calendar.

You Are Not a Machine

Let's say this loud and clear:

- You don't have to earn rest.

- You're not "falling behind" for needing a day off.

- Productivity does not determine your worth.

You're a human being living through a rigorous, demanding process.

That means your needs will change. Your energy will fluctuate. Your buckets will shift. And your job isn't to get it perfect. Your job is to *keep coming back to yourself*.

That's what integration is. That's what #GRADBOSS living looks like.

Chapter Eleven

Cultivating Supportive Relationships

Whether it's friends, family, partners, or peers—relationships matter. We'll cover boundaries, communication, and what support actually looks like.

You are not meant to do grad school alone.

Even if you're an introvert.Even if your program feels isolating. Even if it feels like no one in your life really understands what you're going through.

Relationships are one of the most powerful resources you have in grad school. But they don't just *happen*. They have to be cultivated, protected, and sometimes reimagined to fit this new chapter of your life.

Let's talk about how to build your support system without overextending yourself, and what to do when the people around you don't fully get it.

Why Relationships Matter More Than You Think

When you're knee-deep in deadlines, it can be tempting to retreat into your own little academic bubble. But isolation is dangerous in grad school. It leads to:

- More self-doubt

- More burnout

- More rumination

- And less joy

You don't need a huge circle. You just need the right people in your corner. People who:

- Celebrate your wins

- Encourage your growth

- Remind you of who you are outside of academia

- Support your boundaries without guilt

Relationships like that don't just make grad school easier. They make it *worth it*.

Recalibrating Existing Relationships

Let's start with the people already in your life (family, friends, partners) who knew you before grad school began.

They may not understand academia. They might think you're "just in school" or wonder why you're so stressed all the time.

That's okay. The goal isn't to make them experts in your field. The goal is to help them understand *how to support you*.

Here's what helps:

- **Communicate your schedule clearly** – Let them know when you're most busy and when you're available to connect.

- **Explain the stakes** – If you're working toward a big milestone (like comps or a dissertation chapter), give them a simple explanation of why it matters and how they can help.

- **Ask for the support you need** – Be specific. "Can we do a no-school talk dinner this weekend?" or "I'd love a quick pep talk before my presentation."

It's okay if people don't fully understand what you're doing. What matters is whether they're *willing* to understand you.

Building New Relationships in Grad School

Grad school friendships are unique. You're often thrown together with people who are wildly different from you, and yet, deeply connected by the shared challenge of academic life.

If you've struggled to make new connections, try this:

- **Start small** – Say yes to a group study session or coffee with a peer after class.

- **Find common ground** – Ask about hobbies, weekend plans, or how they're organizing their workload.

- **Show up consistently** – Join a campus club, writing group, or online community where other grad students gather.

- **Be the one who invites** – Start a co-working session, send a funny meme, or plan a snack break between lectures.

You don't have to become best friends overnight. Grad school community is built moment by moment.

Setting Boundaries in Relationships

Here's where it gets tricky: some relationships, even well-meaning ones, can drain you.

Maybe it's:

- A peer who always vents but never asks how you're doing

- A family member who pressures you to succeed without understanding your world

- A partner who doesn't respect your need for study time

This is where boundaries come in.

A boundary is not a wall. It's a bridge.

It's how you communicate what you need in order to stay well.

Here's how to start:

- **Name what's not working** – What behavior is making it hard for you to thrive?

- **Decide what you need** – More space? More clarity? More support?

- **Communicate clearly** – "I can't talk during work hours, but I'd love to catch up on Sunday." / "I'm feeling overwhelmed. Can we do something fun this weekend without talking about school?"

Boundaries are a form of care for you *and* for your relationships.

Check In: Who's in Your Circle?

Grab a pen or open your Notes app. Write down:
- 2–3 people who make you feel seen and supported

- 1 person you want to reconnect with

- 1 relationship that needs a new boundary

This check-in isn't about judgment. It's about *awareness.* Knowing your support system helps you lean on it when things get hard and helps you notice when it's time to grow or shift it.

#GRADBOSS Reminder: Support Looks Different for Everyone

For some, support looks like a standing Sunday dinner with family. For others, it's a group text with meme exchanges and pep talks. For others still, it's a quiet online community where you don't have to explain yourself.

There's no right way to feel supported. The only question is: *What kind of support helps you feel most like yourself?*

That's the one to prioritize.

You Deserve People Who Get It

You deserve to be supported. Encouraged. Celebrated. Not just for your academic work, but for who you are as a human being.

Whether your circle is big or small, in person or online, new or lifelong—let it be intentional. Let it be yours.

Grad school is hard. But with the right people in your corner? You don't just survive it.

You rise.

Chapter Twelve

Building Your Grad School Community

You don't have to do this alone. Here's how to find your people on campus, in town, and online.

There's a myth in grad school that you're supposed to be a lone genius.

You know the image: A brilliant, overworked student scribbling notes in isolation, fueled by caffeine and grit.

But here's what #GRADBOSSes understand: No one gets through grad school alone. Not the ones who look like they have it all together. Not even the ones who finish early.

Behind every successful grad student is a network. It may be tiny or sprawling, local or virtual, but it exists. And if yours doesn't yet, that's what this chapter is for.

Why Community Matters

When you're in a challenging program, surrounded by people who seem like they never struggle, it's easy to shrink inward. To assume you're the only one confused, overwhelmed, or behind.

But community flips the script. It says:

- *You're not the only one.*

- *You're not behind.*

- *You're doing hard things and others are doing them too.*

A strong grad school community can help you:

- Share resources and information

- Stay accountable on long-term projects

- Feel seen, heard, and understood

- Celebrate your wins (especially the tiny ones)

- Reduce burnout and isolation

- Build relationships that last long after graduation

Where to Find Your People

Community doesn't always appear in obvious places. Sometimes, you have to build it yourself (or notice what's already there).

Here are a few places to start:

On Campus

- Your cohort or lab group

- Graduate student organizations

- Departmental committees or volunteer roles

- Writing groups or journal clubs

- Graduate student lounges or workspaces

If nothing exists yet? Create it. Start a co-working group or a coffee hour. Others are likely craving connection, too.

Online Spaces

- Grad student X (formerly Twitter) / Threads / LinkedIn

- #AcademicTwitter, #PhDLife, #GradSchoolStruggles

- Online writing retreats or productivity sprints

- The #GRADBOSS Learning Community (check the Resources section for how to join!)

- Discord or Slack channels for academic fields

Virtual community is just as valid as in-person. Especially for underrepresented students, online spaces can provide affirmation and solidarity you might not find locally.

Beyond Academia

- Faith groups, gyms, art classes, or other interest-based communities

- Book clubs or co-working spaces

- Family and friends from home

You're still allowed to have a life outside of grad school. In fact, it makes you a better student.

How to Build Connection (Even if You're Nervous)

If the idea of "putting yourself out there" makes you anxious, you're not alone. Many grad students feel nervous about initiating friendships or joining new groups.

Here's how to ease in:

- **Start small** – Smile. Make eye contact. Sit next to someone new. Ask how their semester's going.

- **Look for bridges** – Shared classes, common research interests, similar schedules.

- **Be consistent** – Show up to the same events, meetings, or online spaces regularly.

- **Invite, don't wait** – Ask a classmate to grab coffee or study together. Extend the invitation you're hoping to receive.

Community vs. Comparison

Here's something important: **Being in community is not the same as being in competition.**

Yes, you'll meet people who are further along than you. Who seem more confident. Who publish more. Who speak up more. That doesn't mean you don't belong.

Comparison is a thief. Community is a mirror.

It reminds you: *you're not alone, and you're not behind.* When you stop competing and start connecting, everything changes.

#GRADBOSS Tip: Build a Micro-Community

You don't need 10 best friends. You need 2–3 solid connections who make you feel safe, supported, and seen.

These are your **accountability buddies**. Your **emergency pep talkers**. Your **"send help I just cried in my advisor's office" crew.**

Start with one. Be the first to check in. Send a meme. Share a resource. Ask how they're doing. These micro-communities are the backbone of your #GRADBOSS experience.

How to Stay Connected When You're Busy

When midterms hit or your dissertation deadline is looming, connection often falls to the bottom of the list. But even then, small actions count:

- Send a 2-minute voice note to check in

- React to a classmate's post or win

- Drop a funny meme in a group chat

- Share your schedule and invite others to co-work with you

Community doesn't have to mean constant availability. It just means *intentional presence.*

You Deserve Connection

You were not meant to power through grad school on your own. You deserve friendship. Support. Encouragement. Real connection.

Whether your community is one person or a whole cohort, virtual or in person, formal or informal—it counts.

Don't wait for the perfect moment to find your people. Start with the ones who are already showing up. And keep showing up, too.

Because thriving in grad school isn't just about strategy. It's about *belonging*.

Chapter Thirteen

Navigating Advisor & Faculty Relationships

*H*ow to choose (or change) an advisor, prepare for meetings, and maintain your confidence in power-imbalanced spaces.

In grad school, no relationship impacts your experience quite like the one you have with your advisor. They might be your biggest advocate, your toughest critic, your main source of feedback, or all three at once.

And while many grad students have supportive, encouraging advisors, others face misalignment, poor communication, or outright harm.

Whatever your experience looks like, one truth remains: **You are not powerless in this relationship.**

You can learn to navigate it with strategy, clarity, and confidence.

The Power Dynamics Are Real

Let's name it up front. Advisor and faculty relationships exist within systems of power. Your advisor may:

- Approve your thesis or dissertation

- Recommend you for funding or conferences

- Shape how others in your department see you

- Influence your sense of worth and academic identity

That's a lot. Especially if you're from an underrepresented group, or you don't feel like you "fit" the mold of a "typical" grad student in your field.

It's easy to shrink yourself to keep the peace. To second-guess your ideas, delay asking for help, or tolerate mistreatment. But a healthy advisor relationship doesn't require you to sacrifice your sense of self. It requires boundaries, communication, and support.

Let's walk through it together.

Choosing the Right Advisor (or Reassessing One)

If you're early in your program and haven't yet selected an advisor, here are some questions to consider:

Values & Mentorship Style

- Do they support students with similar goals or backgrounds as mine?

- Are they collaborative or more hands-off?

- Do they make time for students or seem constantly unavailable?

Communication
- Are they clear and respectful in their feedback?

- Do they answer emails or requests within a reasonable time-frame?

Support Systems
- Do their current students seem supported and successful?

- Do they advocate for students at the departmental level?

Vibes Matter
- Do I feel respected when I speak with them?

- Do I feel like I can ask questions and be myself?

If you're further along and realizing something isn't working—pause and reflect. It's never too late to adjust boundaries or seek a new advisor if needed.

Preparing for Advisor Meetings

Advisor meetings can feel high-stakes, especially if your advisor has a strong personality or expects you to "just know" how things work.

Here's how to take control of the meeting, even when you're nervous:

Before the Meeting:

- Review what you've worked on since your last meeting

- Identify 2–3 things you want feedback on

- List any questions or blockers

- Update your progress tracker (or draft a brief agenda)

During the Meeting:

- Take notes or bring a printed agenda

- Summarize their feedback aloud: "So what I'm hearing is…"

- Confirm next steps and expectations

- Don't be afraid to ask for clarification

After the Meeting:

- Send a quick summary email: "Here's what I'll be working on and when I'll check in next."

- Reflect: What went well? What could I do differently next time?

You'll find a printable Advisor Meeting Template in the Resources section to help you stay organized and confident.

When Things Get Difficult

Sometimes, the advisor-student relationship breaks down. You might experience:

- Dismissive or degrading feedback

- Pressure to work unreasonable hours

- Delayed or inconsistent communication

- Misalignment on research goals or expectations

- Bias, discrimination, or microaggressions

If this is your situation, you are not alone and you are not stuck.

Here's what to do:

1. **Document everything** – Save emails, write down dates and summaries of meetings.

2. **Talk to someone you trust** – Another faculty member, program director, or graduate coordinator.

3. **Know your rights and policies** – Your graduate school likely has grievance procedures or ombudspersons available.

4. **Explore your options** – You *can* switch advisors or add a co-advisor. It's more common than you think.

I've worked with multiple grad students who had to switch advisors because of misalignment. And none of them regretting their decision, even if it pushed their graduation date back a year. Peace, support, and confidence as you complete your degree are worth the delay.

You don't need to suffer in silence. You deserve mentorship that supports, not sabotages, your growth.

Faculty Relationships Beyond Your Advisor

Don't limit your network to a single mentor. Build a **"constellation of mentors"**—a group of faculty, staff, or professionals who each support you in different ways.

Your constellation might include:

- A writing center director who helps with structure and flow

- A librarian who knows your field's databases inside and out

- A professor in another department who shares your identity or research lens

- A staff member who checks in and cheers you on

The more people in your corner, the more resilience you build throughout your grad school experience..

#GRADBOSS Step: Advocate for Yourself

No matter where you are in your grad school journey, you are allowed to:

- Ask for what you need

- Say when something isn't working

- Change your mind

- Redefine what mentorship means for you

This is *your* academic experience. Your advisor is part of it, but they are not the whole thing.

You Deserve Respect & Support

The advisor relationship can be one of the most challenging parts of grad school, but it can also be one of the most transformative. Whether your relationship is smooth or rocky, nurturing or strained, you're not powerless.

You can prepare. You can pivot. You can set boundaries. You can lead.

Because at the end of the day, you're not just here to earn a degree. You're here to grow into the version of yourself who knows how to navigate hard things with clarity and confidence.

Need help finding the words?

If you're not sure how to reach out to your advisor, set a boundary, or request a change, turn to the *Bonus Email Scripts* in the Resources & Reflections section at the back of this book.

You'll find sample messages for navigating tough conversations with clarity and confidence. Because advocating for yourself doesn't have to mean doing it alone.

And that? That is a *#GRADBOSS* move.

Part V: Keep Going

When things get hard and how to make it worth it.

Chapter Fourteen

Failure Is Part of the Process

*E*very grad student fails. The secret is in how you respond. We'll walk through common failure moments and how to recover and reframe.

Let's start with the most important point: **Failure in grad school is not optional. It's inevitable.**

Everyone fails at something. Yes, even the students you admire most. The ones who publish early. The ones who seem confident and collected. The ones who present at conferences with ease.

But we don't talk about failure. And because we don't talk about it, it feels like it's only happening to you.

It's not.

Failure is built into the grad school process. It's how you grow. It's how you learn what kind of scholar (and person) you want to be.

Let's Normalize It

Failure in grad school doesn't always look dramatic. It's not always failing a class (though that happens too).

It might look like:

- Not finishing a paper on time

- Getting rejected from a fellowship or journal

- Struggling to understand a key concept

- Feeling totally lost in your research

- Messing up a presentation

- Missing a major deadline

- Getting called out in class or during a lab meeting

- Receiving harsh feedback on something you worked hard on

And the hardest part? Failure in grad school doesn't just feel like a mistake. It feels personal. Like a reflection of your intelligence or your worth.

That's why we have to name it. Talk about it. Learn how to face it and move through it.

My Own Failure: The Incomplete That Changed Everything

If you've read earlier chapters, you know that my very first semester in grad school did *not* go according to plan.

I earned an **incomplete** in one of my core courses—Topology. Not because I didn't try. But because I wasn't ready for that level of content yet.

I had never taken topology before. It was confusing, abstract, and completely new to me. I failed one of the major exams. My professor posted a list of scores on the board: pass on one side, fail on the other. My score was on the fail side.

Although, I was one of the top scorers on *that* side. It was crushing.

But that moment, getting the incomplete, spending the entire next semester proving theorems one-on-one with my professor, crying through the process, taught me something essential:

This is how you learn upper-level math. And this is how you survive grad school failure:

- By taking the lesson without letting it define you

- By facing the hard part instead of running from it

- By believing in your ability to keep going

That incomplete changed how I approached everything that came after. And I never got another C again.

How to Recover from a Failure Spiral

When something goes wrong, your nervous system goes into over-drive. You might feel shame, panic, exhaustion, or the urge to disappear. Here's a framework for moving through it:

Step 1: Pause & Breathe

Don't try to fix everything right away. Give yourself time to feel what you feel. Breathe. Step away if you need to.

Step 2: Find the Facts

What *actually* happened? Separate the facts from the feelings. E.g., "I missed the deadline" is a fact. "I'm a failure who doesn't belong here" is a thought.

Step 3: Name the Trigger

Did this failure hit your perfectionism? Your fear of disappointing others? Your fear of not being good enough?

Knowing your trigger helps you respond instead of react.

Step 4: Talk to Someone

Text a friend. Visit office hours. Reach out to a peer or mentor. Say: "Hey, something didn't go well. Can I talk it through?"

Shame thrives in silence. Speaking it out loud helps loosen its grip.

Step 5: Reframe & Regroup

Ask yourself:

- What did I learn from this?

- What will I do differently next time?

- What support do I need moving forward?

Then, take one small action. Just one. Send the email. Open the document. Show up.

That one step is how you begin again.

What Failure Isn't

Failure isn't proof that you're not smart. It's not a signal to drop out. It's not the end of your story.

Grad school is designed to stretch you, and that means you'll hit your edge. The goal isn't to avoid every mistake. It's to build a system that can *carry you* when things go wrong.

That's the #GRADBOSS way.

#GRADBOSS Reframe: What If This Isn't a Detour?

What if this moment of failure is part of your path, not a detour from it? What if it's not about falling—but about *rising again with new tools*? What if the person you're becoming is someone who knows how to bend without breaking?

That's a powerful kind of success. And no exam, grade, or missed deadline can take that from you.

Permission to Keep Going

You're allowed to have bad days. You're allowed to mess up. You're allowed to take a breath, ask for help, and try again.

Failure doesn't define you. *Your response does.*

So the next time you stumble, remember: This is part of the process. You're still on your path. You're still a #GRADBOSS.

Chapter Fifteen

Fulfillment, Joy & The Life Beyond the Degree

*G*rad school is not your whole life. Here's how to find joy now, not just "after graduation," and build a life you're proud of.

Let's zoom out for a moment.

You started grad school with a reason. Maybe it was curiosity, a long-time dream, a mentor who believed in you, or a career goal you're chasing. Maybe you're still figuring that part out (and that's okay too).

I didn't figure out what I would do as a career until my third year of my PhD program after teaching for the first time.

But somewhere along the way, it's easy to forget that this is just one chapter in your life.

You are a whole person. With desires and hobbies and relationships and a future that stretches far beyond your program.

So let's talk about something academia rarely mentions: **Joy. Fulfillment. And the life you want to live when the degree is done.**

Don't Wait to Be Happy

There's a quiet myth that floats through every grad school hallway:

"When I finish this paper... when I pass this exam... when I defend... THEN I'll feel proud. Then I'll feel free."

The grad school truth: there is no magical finish line where everything suddenly feels good.

Joy doesn't live on the other side of productivity. Fulfillment doesn't wait for you at graduation. You have to create space for those things now.

Even in the middle of coursework. Even in research chaos. Even when you feel behind.

Redefine What Success Means to You

Take a moment and ask yourself:

- What do I want my life to *feel* like, not just look like on paper?

- What do I want to be known for beyond my title or CV?

- What kind of impact do I want to make, and on whom?

- What values do I want to guide me, even after grad school is over?

These aren't soft questions. They're strategic ones. Because when you're clear on your definition of success, you stop chasing someone else's. You start living *your* version of a meaningful life.

What Joy Looks Like in Real Life

Joy isn't always fireworks or Instagram-worthy moments. Sometimes it's a quiet morning with your favorite tea. A walk without headphones. A belly laugh with your cohort. A moment where you feel, just for a second, *like yourself again.*

Let yourself have those moments.

Schedule joy the way you schedule meetings. Prioritize peace the way you prioritize deadlines. It's not a distraction from your work. It's what sustains it.

The Bigger Picture

Grad school is a powerful chapter but it is not your whole story. One day, this degree will just be a line on your résumé or CV. But the habits, values, and self-trust you're building right now? Those will follow you into every next step.

Into careers. Into families. Into friendships. Into impact that ripples far beyond what your advisor sees.

You're not just earning a credential. You're becoming the kind of person who shows up with purpose, leads with clarity, and lives with intention.

The #GRADBOSS Mindset: In Their Words

Grad school doesn't come with a roadmap, but it does come with community. Throughout this book, you've heard from students just like you: ambitious, overwhelmed, determined, and growing. Each of them has faced setbacks, found their rhythm, and redefined what success means on their own terms.

So before you close this book and head back into your semester, we wanted to leave you with one last reminder:

There's no single way to be a #GRADBOSS.

It's not about perfection. It's about *intention*.

It's about returning to your values when the pressure mounts, and creating systems that support (not suffocate) your success.

Here's what being a #GRADBOSS means to some of the students I've had the joy of working with. May their words remind you that you're not alone and that your version of thriving is more than enough.

Cristina

"Being a #GRADBOSS means creating your own definition of success—and then owning it."

Cristina came to grad school with deep clarity about her "why." For her, it wasn't about chasing someone else's version of achievement—it was about alignment. That focus helped her move through challenges with purpose, even when things got tough.

Asha

"Being a #GRADBOSS is about self-care, reflection, and the freedom to decide what you need—and when you need it."

Asha connected the #GRADBOSS identity to *flexibility and intentional reflection*. She described it as giving yourself permission to take breaks, make space for your real life, and still move forward with clarity. For her, being a boss means checking in regularly, adjusting when needed, and remembering that rest and honesty fuel real success.

Lynn

"It's someone who's not just surviving grad school, but thriving through it—on their own terms."

For Lynn, thriving meant setting boundaries and building habits that actually worked for his life, not just his program. He defined success by sustainability, not struggle.

Addie

"A #GRADBOSS knows when to rest, when to speak up, and when to ask for help."

Addie's definition of being a #GRADBOSS was about *self-awareness*. She learned to protect her energy, use her voice, and reach out before burnout hit. It wasn't always easy, but it changed everything.

Asya

"It's about leading yourself, even when things feel messy."

For Asya, grad school brought both brilliance and chaos. Her #GRADBOSS mindset helped her stay grounded—, specially when things felt out of control. She leaned into progress over perfection and trusted her capacity to adapt.

Briana

"Being a #GRADBOSS means staying focused on your why and not losing yourself in the process."

Briana described her journey as one of reflection and resilience. Whenever things got confusing, she came back to her "why." That inner compass helped her stay steady, even when the academic path felt uncertain.

#GRADBOSS Reflection: Write Your Vision

Take a moment to imagine your life five years from now. What are you doing? Who are you surrounded by? How do your days feel?

Now, ask: What can I do *this semester* to move in that direction? Maybe it's setting a boundary.Maybe it's exploring a non-academic path.Maybe it's finding joy outside your work.

Whatever it is, your future self will thank you.

A Final Word

You don't have to become someone else to succeed in grad school. You can be brilliant and burned out. You can be ambitious and still need rest. You can lead with softness and still change the world.

You already belong here. You've already come so far.

And this book? It's just a reminder. To protect your peace. To trust your growth. To lead your life (not just your academic journey) with intention.

You're not just surviving grad school. You're becoming a *#GRAD-BOSS.*

Another Letter
from the Author

D ear #GRADBOSS,

     If no one's told you this lately, let me be the first: **I am so proud of you.**

Whether you're just beginning your program, finishing up your degree, or somewhere in the messy, magical middle, you've already done something courageous by choosing this path. You've committed to your growth, your goals, and your future. And that's worth celebrating.

Writing this second edition of *#GRADBOSS: A Grad School Survival Guide* was my way of sitting beside you and saying,

"You don't have to do this alone."

I created this book to be the guide I wish I had when I was in your shoes. But I also know that books are just the beginning. What really changes your grad school experience is connection. Community. Stories. Knowing that your voice, your experience, and your dreams *matter.*

So if this book has resonated with you, I want to invite you deeper into the #GRADBOSS community.

Start with the Grad School Stories podcast. Each episode features real grad students sharing their journeys—the good, the hard, the surprising, and the transformational. You'll hear what it's *really* like and leave each story reminded that you belong.

Join the #GRADBOSS Learning Community. This is your cozy corner of the internet. A place to plan your weeks, connect with others, attend virtual coworking sessions, and get support through every stage of grad school. Inside, you'll find workshops, planning tools, accountability check-ins, and a whole community cheering you on.

Share this book with your grad school friends. If this guide helped you feel more grounded, confident, or seen, don't keep it to yourself. Recommend it to your cohort, share it in your group chat, or pass it along to the next incoming class. We rise together.

All the links, bonuses, and resources mentioned throughout the book (including sample email scripts, planning templates, and exclusive extras) can be found at:

theacademicsociety.com/gradboss-book-gifts

Thank you for reading. Thank you for showing up. And thank you for trusting me to walk alongside you on this journey.

Here's to progress with purpose and a life beyond the degree that feels like *yours.*

With gratitude and #GRADBOSS pride,

Dr. Toyin Alli

Author of *#GRADBOSS*, Founder of The Academic Society

Resources & Reflections

G rad school can feel overwhelming, but you don't have to do it alone—and you don't have to start from scratch. These resources are here to help you turn the strategies in this book into simple systems, routines, and supports you can actually use.

Whether you're planning your week, preparing for an advisor meeting, or writing a hard email, these tools are designed to give you structure *without* the stress.

You'll find printable versions of everything below at: **theacadem icsociety.com/gradboss-book-gifts**

Weekly Planning & Reflection Worksheets

Grad school moves fast—but your time still belongs to you. These pages are designed to help you pause, reflect, and plan your week with purpose. Each sheet includes:

- A Weekly Overview

- Space to set your anchor goals

- Midweek check-in + end-of-week reflection

- Notes section for wins, pivots, or reminders

You can print them, reuse them, or build a rhythm around them. The goal? Progress without burnout.

Grad School Confidence Starter Kit

A workbook to help you feel more grounded, capable, and in control. Inside you'll find:

- An example of a productive weekly schedule using **Productivity Chunks**

- A space to design your own ideal week

- Prompts to clarify your **non-negotiables** and set boundaries

- A "Start Strong" checklist to reset your semester

This is your go-to toolkit when you need a fresh start or a reminder that you've got this.

Advisor Meeting Template

No more awkward silences or "What should I say?" moments. This template helps you prep for meetings with your advisor or committee so you can show up confidently and make the most of your time together. Includes:

- A meeting prep checklist

- Prompts for updates, questions, and action items

- Space to track your progress across the semester

Perfect for your first meeting or for those mid-semester touchpoints that sneak up on you.

Sample Email Scripts

Sometimes, finding the right words is the hardest part. These editable scripts are here to help you advocate for yourself with clarity and professionalism.

Includes templates for:

- Requesting a meeting or extension

- Setting a boundary

- Following up after silence

- Navigating tough advisor dynamics

- Requesting support or changing course

You'll find the full script library in your downloadable resource bundle.

Grad School Stories – Private Podcast

Real interviews. Real students. Real talk.Listen to stories from the #GRADBOSS Learning Community and discover what thriving *really* looks like in grad school.

The #GRADBOSS Learning Community

Join our cozy corner of the internet. Connect with fellow students, attend co-working sessions, ask questions, and stay encouraged all semester long.

All Downloads + Templates

Get access to everything in this section (plus a few extras!): theacademicsociety.com/gradboss-book-gifts

How to Use This Book With a Grad Cohort (For Educators)

T hank you for supporting your students not only as scholars, but as whole people.

This book was written to meet grad students where they are—overwhelmed, ambitious, and often unsure how to navigate the unspoken rules of graduate education. It's not just a survival guide. It's a mindset and planning toolkit designed to help students feel *confident, capable, and connected* to their purpose.

If you're an educator, mentor, or program director, here are a few ways you can use this book to support your graduate cohort:

Assign as a Cohort-Wide Resource

Provide this book to your full incoming class (or a targeted group of scholars) and use it to set the tone for their grad school experience.

Many programs gift it at orientation, or during summer bridge/prep programming.

Use Chapters as Monthly Themes

The chapters are grouped into five sections that naturally lend themselves to a semester-long series:

- **Part I: Own Your Experience** → *Start-of-semester identity + confidence work*

- **Part II: Plan With Purpose** → *Goal setting + time management modules*

- **Part III: Get Stuff Done (Without Losing Yourself)** → *Productivity, focus, research*

- **Part IV: Real Life in Grad School** → *Wellness, relationships, and community*

- **Part V: Keep Going** → *Resilience + life beyond the degree*

You can assign one section per month and discuss during cohort meetings or professional development sessions.

Host Reflective Discussions

Use the built-in student spotlights and end-of-chapter prompts to spark meaningful conversation. Students can share:

- What part of the chapter resonated most

- Which tools they've tried implementing

- What they're struggling with and how others might support them

You don't have to lead with lectures. The book is designed to prompt vulnerability and shared reflection.

Pair With the Included Tools

Each copy of the book comes with access to:
- Printable planning templates

- Advisor meeting prep worksheets

- Weekly and monthly reflection pages

- Sample email scripts for common situations

- A private podcast (Grad School Stories) with student interviews

You can encourage students to use these tools between meetings, or as part of structured cohort programming.

Everything is available at:**theacademicsociety.com/gradboss-book-gifts**

Bring Me In for Guest Support

I offer a variety of guest experiences to deepen the #GRADBOSS transformation for your cohort:

- **Live Virtual Workshops** (popular topics: time management, impostor syndrome, productivity)

- **Strategic Planning Sessions** (start-of-semester or mid-semester refreshers)

- **Train-the-Trainer** sessions for mentors and advisors

- **Bulk discounts + customized programming** for institutions and fellowships

To collaborate or request a speaking engagement, visit **theacademicsociety.com/speaking**

A Final Note to Mentors & Educators

The students reading this book are in a pivotal moment of identity formation, not just as academics, but as humans. Your willingness to invest in their holistic success is powerful.

Thank you for believing in your students' potential, and for trusting this book as a companion on their journey. Together, we can change the culture of grad school, one confident, joyful, empowered student at a time.

— **Dr. Toyin Alli**